PLANES

Frances Ridley

Copyright © ticktock Entertainment Ltd 2007
First published in Great Britain in 2007 by ticktock Media Ltd.,
The Old Sawmill, 103 Goods Station Road,
Tunbridge Wells, Kent, TN1 2DP

ticktock project editor: Julia Adams
ticktock project designer: Emma Randall

We would like to thank: Alix Wood.

ISBN 978 1 84696 560 9

Printed in China
9 8 7 6 5 4

Picture credits:
b=bottom; c=centre; t=top; r=right; l=left
Aviation Picture Library: 3, 6-7, 8-9c, 10-11, 12-13, 14-15, 16-17, back cover cr; Corbis: 2, 4-5, 9t,
20-21, back cover cl; NASA: 18-19, 22-23.

Every effort has been made to trace the copyright holders,
and we apologise in advance for any unintentional omissions.
We would be pleased to insert the appropriate acknowledgements
in any subsequent edition of this publication.

Contents

Airbus A380

The Airbus A380 is the largest airliner in the world. It has two engines on each wing. It carries 853 passengers.

The Airbus A380 has three decks. One deck is for **cargo**. The other two decks are for passengers.

There are shops and places to eat on the Airbus. There are places for children to play, too!

A380

SR-71 Blackbird

The SR-71 Blackbird is a spy plane. It carries cameras and **sensors**. The cameras are used to spy on the enemy. The sensors are used to spot enemy planes.

The Blackbird has powerful engines and is very fast. Its top speed is 3,621 km/h.

6

The plane is made from a special metal. This keeps the plane cool when it goes very fast.

Boeing 747

Boeing launched the 747 in 1966. At that time, passenger planes had one aisle of seats. The 747 has two aisles of seats. It was called the 'Jumbo Jet' because it was so big!

Modern
Boeing 747s
also carry
cargo. The
747-400F has a
nose that lifts up.
You load the cargo through the nose!

B-2 Spirit

The B-2 Spirit is a **stealth aircraft.**
It is almost invisible to **radar**.

The B-2 looks like a giant wing. Its skin is black and smooth. The bulges hide the engines, cockpit and bombs.

The B-2's top speed is 1,013 km/h. It makes less noise than normal planes.

Eurofighter Typhoon

The Eurofighter Typhoon is a warplane. It carries a gun, **missiles** and bombs.

Most of the Typhoon's body is made of **carbon fibre**. Carbon fibre is light. It keeps the plane cool at high speeds.

The Typhoon's top speed is 2,129 km/h. It has two engines. It can take off in only five seconds!

F117A Nighthawk

The Nighthawk is a bomber.
Its top speed is 1,126 km/h.

The Nighthawk's strange shape
breaks up **radar** signals.
This makes the Nighthawk
hard to spot!

14

The Nighthawk doesn't need to land
for more fuel. It can be filled up while
it is flying. A tanker aircraft links up to
the Nighthawk. It pumps in the fuel
through a hose.

Harrier Jump Jet

The Harrier was launched in 1969.
It was the first **VTOL** aircraft. A VTOL
aircraft doesn't need a runway.
It can take off and land from a ship,
a forest clearing or a park!

The Harrier has a special design. It can change direction very fast. This makes it hard to follow and chase.

Space Shuttle

The Space Shuttle takes people and satellites to space. A huge fuel tank launches the Shuttle. Then it uses fuel from two rocket **boosters**. The rocket boosters fall off when they are empty.

Enterprise

United S

The Shuttle gets very hot
when it comes back to
Earth. Special tiles
help to keep it cool.
The Shuttle lands on
a runway. A huge
parachute slows
it down.

Voyager

In 1986, Voyager flew round the world non-stop. No plane had ever done this before.

Voyager looks very strange. Its body is fixed in the middle of two long wings. The body holds all the fuel it needs.

Two people were on board. They had to lie down to fly the plane!

The wings curve upwards when the plane is flying. They scrape the ground when the plane has landed.

X43A

NASA is famous for making space rockets. It also carries out **research** into aircraft.

The X43A has no pilot. It goes too fast for humans to survive.

22

The X43A's top speed is 10,621 km/h.
It could go from London to New York
in just 40 minutes. In a normal plane,
this journey takes seven hours!

The X43A does not
take off from the ground.
It is carried into the sky
underneath a plane and
launched.

This is the X43A on the end of the
Hyper-X rocket that launches it.

Glossary

Boosters	Fuel tanks on the side of a space rocket.
Carbon fibre	Light material used to make planes.
Cargo	Goods carried on planes.
Missiles	Weapon that travels to a target.
Radar	Way of spotting objects that are far away.
Research	Finding out about something.
Satellites	Objects that orbit around the Earth – they collect information.
Sensors	Things that help pilots fly the plane, fire weapons and spot enemy planes.
Stealth aircraft	Planes that cannot be spotted easily.
VTOL	Planes that don't need runways to take off. They can go straight up.

**OFFICE FOR STANDARDS
IN EDUCATION**

THE OFSTED HANDBOOK

Guidance on the Inspection of
NURSERY & PRIMARY SCHOOLS

Issued by Her Majesty's Chief Inspector of Schools in England

London: HMSO

Office for Standards in Education
Alexandra House
29-33 Kingsway
London WC2B 6SE

ISBN 0 11 350066 1

CONTENTS